MUSIC MAKERS

Pianos

by Cynthia Amoroso and Robert B. Noyed

Watch her hands move quickly back and forth. She presses down on the **keys**. Plink, plink. Plunk, plunk. She is playing the piano!

The piano is a fun instrument to play.

The piano is a **keyboard** instrument. It has 88 keys. Some are black and some are white.

The piano has more white keys than black keys.

The piano is also a **string instrument**. When a key is pressed, a hammer hits a string inside the piano. The string **vibrates**. The vibration makes a sound.

A piano has more strings than keys.

A piano is played with both hands. Fingers move up and down the keyboard to press the keys. Two parts of a song are played at once—one part with each hand.

The left and right hands can play at the same time.

Each key makes a different sound. The left keys sound low. The right keys sound high. A player touches a key softly to make a soft sound. A player pushes harder for a loud sound.

The piano can sound soft or loud.

Piano players use their feet, too. They pump the **pedals** underneath the piano. Pedals change the piano's sounds.

Pianos have two or three pedals.

The first piano was made about 300 years ago in Italy. Now, pianos are played all over the world.

Some piano players travel the world to play.

Many schools and homes have pianos. Many children take piano lessons. They practice pressing the keys.

Children can start piano lessons at a very young age.

Some pianos are very large. Some are smaller. The piano makes many kinds of music. Two kinds of music are **classical** and **jazz**.

Many jazz bands have pianos in them.

Plink, plink. Plunk, plunk. Playing the piano is very fun!

Piano players read sheet music.

Glossary

classical (KLASS-uh-kul): Classical is a type of music that includes opera and chamber music. Classical music can be played on the piano.

jazz (JAZ): Jazz is a type of music that is lively and rhythmic. Jazz music can be played on the piano.

keyboard (KEE-bord): All the keys on a piano are called a keyboard. A keyboard has black and white keys.

keys (KEEZ): Keys are the black and white bars on a piano. A player presses the keys to make sounds.

pedals (PED-ullz): Pedals are levers on a piano that you push with your feet. Pedals change the piano's sound.

string instrument (STRING IN-struh-munt): A string instrument is an instrument that makes sound by pressing or plucking strings. The piano is a string instrument.

vibrates (VY-brayts): Something that moves back and forth very quickly vibrates. When piano strings vibrate, they make a sound.

To Find Out More

Books

Currie, Stephen. *Pianos*. San Diego, CA: Blackbirch Press, 2006.

Houston, Scott. *Play Piano in a Flash—for Kids!* New York: Hyperion, 2005.

Kril, Christine Bemko. *I Can Do It! Piano Book: First Book of Favorite Songs*. Fredericksburg, VA: Kapok, 2005.

Web Sites

Visit our Web site for links about pianos:
childsworld.com/links

Note to Parents, Teachers, and Librarians: We routinely verify our Web links to make sure they are safe and active sites. So encourage your readers to check them out!

Index

About the Authors

Cynthia Amoroso has worked as an elementary school teacher and a high school English teacher. Writing children's books is another way for her to share her passion for the written word.

Robert B. Noyed has worked as a newspaper reporter and in the communications department for a Minnesota school district. He enjoys the challenge and accomplishment of writing children's books.

On the cover: Playing the piano takes practice.

Published by The Child's World®
1980 Lookout Drive • Mankato, MN 56003-1705
800-599-READ • www.childsworld.com

ACKNOWLEDGMENTS
The Child's World®: Mary Berendes, Publishing Director
The Design Lab: Design and production
Red Line Editorial: Editorial direction

PHOTO CREDITS: Chris Scredon/iStockphoto, cover; iStockphoto, cover;
Alex Ptemkin/iStockphoto, 3; Dejan Ljami /123rf, 5; Big Stock Photo,
7, 13, 15; Yenwen Lu/iStockphoto, 9; Rob Cruse/iStockphoto, 11; Noam
Armonn/123rf, 17; Vincenzo Vergelli/iStockphoto, 19; Serge Shutov/Big
Stock Photo, 21

Printed in the United States of America in Mankato, Minnesota.
November 2009
F11460

LIBRARY OF CONGRESS CATALOGING-IN-PUBLICATION DATA
Amoroso, Cynthia.
  Pianos / by Cynthia Amoroso and Robert B. Noyed.
     p. cm. — (Music makers)
  Includes index.
  ISBN 978-1-60253-355-4 (library bound : alk. paper)
  1. Piano—Juvenile literature. I. Noyed, Robert B. II. Title. III. Series.
  ML650.A48 2010
  786.5'19—dc22   2009030207